What's Your Excuse?

Be a Goal Getter!

By Karen Grosz

What's Your Excuse?

This book is lovingly dedicated to the man who always encourages me to try the next thing. Thank you, Paul for 30 years of growth and happiness. Karen

Begin as a group. End as a team!

CANVAS CREEK
TEAM BUILDING

Table of Contents

Dear Reader,

This book has been in my life, and on the Amazon shelf, for several years now. It wasn't a best seller, but I've used it in countless ways, with many people.

This update fixes some grammar errors- the type several edits did not catch, and fixes format issues so I can print this little gem- one of those tasks I have procrastinated completing.

I'm telling you these things because I am not perfect and I hope I never give you the impression I think I am. I am human. I set goals. I procrastinate. I do the next thing. I have big dreams and never enough time, just like you.

What I hold closest is my own excuse for success- Figuring it out and working damn hard.

Enjoy this little tome. And buy the next, please. Those purchases are part of my big dream, which is now a goal, and is coming along nicely. Karen 6.17

Chapter 1

The Perfect Excuse

"Watch this." That is what Tony would say as he walked across the showroom snapping his fingers twice, clapping his hands together once and then putting both thumbs in the air, like Fonzie saying "Aye." He'd bound up to the customer, get a little too close, click his heels down on the floor and start to talk. He would talk and talk and talk. Tony always told us he went into sales because he could talk to anyone, about anything.

He loved to demonstrate it too. He'd open his mouth, words would pour forth and pretty soon he'd be smiling. He knew we were watching with rapt attention. What he didn't notice was the customer just standing there, mouth agape. Tony would smile the smile of the performer who is in the middle of his signature 'knock them dead' act.

That act went like this- talk, talk, (never take a breath they can see), talk some more- smile at your co-workers and talk some more.

It really was something to watch.

This man who professed to be a super salesman (I am pretty sure there was a cape involved in that fantasy) would talk until he had told the customer every detail about the car we represented. Mileage, color choices, how many radio pre-set buttons it came with, where the factory was and how lucky they were to get him, Super Salesman, because he was about to take them for a test drive that would blow their minds. It was at this point the customer would have gained enough composure to say, "We are just here for an oil change."

Time after time, I saw Tony take the walk of shame back to salesman row without a test drive, let alone a sale. He could spend up to an hour talking to someone only to find out not only were they not in the market for a new car, a used car, or a new salesman, not even Super Salesman could interest them in the car he wanted them to buy. We will never know, of course, how many of those people went across the street or down the road to another car dealer, found a sales person they could talk *with* and purchased a car that very day.

However, I can tell you one thing. It was never Tony's fault. He'd say, "Those folks had to run to a birthday party." "Those folks were looking for a pick-up, not a sedan." "Those folks didn't have their tax refund yet." "That guy had bad credit."

Tony had as many excuses as he had words and the beauty of his excuse was this: it was never his fault.

They were the problem. *They* had the issue. *They* had walked away. *They* would not listen. *They* were not good customers, at least not the quality he was used to working with.

Tony held tight to the bottom position of the sales chart month after month, but it was never his fault; he was Super Salesman. It was *them.*

Such is the beauty of the perfect excuse. You can tell the excuse over and over, never admitting your role in the failure. *They* are the problem. The weather was bad. The dessert was free. A blister formed at mile three. The packaging is all wrong. The engineers don't know what they are doing. And, lest we forget the most famous excuse of them all, the dog ate the homework.

Excuses are simply little lies told to justify small faults. Maybe you didn't pick up the phone to make sales calls. Maybe you didn't balance the checkbook, take a jog or fix an error.

For some reason, the idea of offering an excuse makes humans feel like we are saving face. The idea that if my story is good enough I will be forgiven seems to be the underlying cause of excuses. As a Christian, I say you are already forgiven, without an excuse -- but that is another topic.

So, are you forgiven when you give an excuse? Usually not. As a matter of fact, not only is forgiveness denied, trust is damaged and self-esteem is jeopardized. None of these are things most people desire or can afford.

In this game of life trust is paramount to success. People want to trust that every word you offer is in their best interest. They expect that what you are telling them is the truth, important to your relationship and relevant to the conversation or any decision being made.

Relationships are won and lost by a slip of the tongue and repeated excuses hinder complete trust. If you make a mistake, miss a goal or a deadline it is much better to say so than damage trust with an excuse for failure.

At work, especially in sales, people are counting on you to deliver what you promised. "The weather was bad" or "my knees get so sore when rain is coming" is not going to cut it. If you have gotten to the point where your supervisor says, "just say excuse number 5" before you even offer your excuse you know your days are numbered and trust has been extinguished.

No matter your profession, little excuses piled on top of one another can tear you down; you begin to doubt yourself. Your expectations become smaller, your goals more distant. As excuses erode your confidence, fear sets in. Work is less fun and you may even begin to find ways to avoid any goal setting at work and possibly look for another, completely different line of work.

If you have the unfathomable delusions of Tony, you can just snap your fingers, say "Watch this," and move to the next customer all the while thinking you are Super Salesman and *they* are the problem. If you live in the real world it might take a bit more than that. You might have to examine your goals, address your excuses, and actually start to achieve your goals.

That is what I will help you to do in this book, be a goal achiever. As you read you will undoubtedly notice I have a love for sales. Many of my stories come from 25 years of actual selling or from coaching sales people and business owners. Over the years, I have come to understand 'sales' is present in many of our normal everyday interactions.

The word selling is a transitive verb which means to make an idea or proposal acceptable to somebody.

With that thought in mind, are you not selling when you say, "It's time for bed, kids?" Is it not sales when the candidate says, "Vote for me!?" I have heard some powerful sales presentations over the need to buy a new couch.

The presentations begin in the living room, often accompanied by a slick sales brochure that falls from the Sunday paper, and are carried all the way to the showroom when the salesman finally takes over.

Because sales are ubiquitous to our experience, the goal setting steps that work for salespeople will work for you. It does not matter if you want to learn to surf, knit, or play the bagpipes. You are going to need to declare your goal, design your plan, and finally commit to being a goal achiever.

The system I will lay out even works even if you are completely afraid of goal setting. I've often worked with people who say "Oh, I never set goals." Or, "I don't know how to set goals." I would argue that those are indeed false statements. If you have ever said, "Self, it is a bit dark in here," then gotten up and turned on a light, you have actually set and achieved a goal. Sure, the goal was simple, to turn on a light, but it is still a goal set and achieved.

Using that idea as a base for confidence you can see that you actually set and achieve a myriad of goals every day. You shower, you feed yourself, you work, you interact with others, you don't run red lights (I hope,) and thus you are able to climb into bed at the end of the day with an impressive set of goals achieved.

If that is where you are starting as a goal setter, then start there. It's okay. For a couple of days list all your small goals achieved. As you more deeply understand that you are indeed a goal setter, you can move forward to the goals that can define a life.

Those defining goals are what we will work on in this book. They are bigger goals -- the sales milestone, the life- long dreams, the physical and mental goals that stand out in your mind and make you feel truly accomplished. It is great to say, "I achieved one hundred and ten goals today including feeding the goldfish!" And so, we will discuss how small goals improve your experience.

I assume, however, that that defining goals are what elude you and are what you hope this book will help you accomplish. It is supremely gratifying to say, "I finally climbed the mountain!" And that is what I want you to be able to do; achieve your defining goal. Time and again I have seen people set the goal to climb the mountain but never actually set out on the journey. Excuses got in their way.

What's Your Excuse?

Chapter 2

You Left That Note on the Table

Several years ago, I announced to God, family, friends, customers, and anyone who would listen that I was going to earn a direct sales company's 20th anniversary trip. It was to be an exclusive cruise. The entire ship would be filled with consultants in the same business I was in -- hundreds of people with the same crazy love of a product and lifestyle, all floating together through the Caribbean.

To say I *had* to be there is an understatement. My business was on fire. The company was growing exponentially and it was one of those serendipitous moments when everything comes together. If I kept doing what I was doing, my success would get me on the trip. Stepping it up just 5% would make earning the trip comfortable as well as rewarding.

I felt confident, not only was I going to be on that cruise, my husband *expected* to be on that cruise. He loved the trips we had earned previously and there was no way he was missing this one. I often joked that if I did not achieve the cruise he would be swimming behind the ship looking for a new consultant. Like my husband, everyone I shared my goal with had the same response, "You can do it!" They really did expect me to have that moment of success.

They were right, I could do it, and I had nine months to accumulate the needed points. The path was simple direct sales business; book events, sell product, recruit others, shampoo, rinse, repeat. I'd been doing sales like this for years, and chances are many of you reading this book know exactly what I am talking about. You represent a product you love and simply offering it to others makes you happy and brings you success. Then, for some reason, I started making excuses.

It snowed. (We lived in Alaska, the only time it didn't snow was when it was getting ready to snow.)

The sun came out. (Now that is a viable excuse- when you live above the 49th parallel and the day is glorious everything work related tends to screech to a halt.)

Company came. I got a cold. I went to lunch. I didn't have time to make calls because I should make dinner...or a quilt...or the bed. You get the idea. I excused myself right up to October, month five of the incentive period. I was so far behind in the accumulation of points I did not deserve to ride in a row boat let alone float blissfully on an exclusive cruise.

I had made excuses not to work, to fall off track, and I knew darn good and well that not one of those excuses would hold up when I stood in front of God and the rest and said "oh, the cruise.... Yeah, well, about that, ... I uh, didn't earn it because..." and that is where I stopped.

Because......? What would my "because" be?

There is a Yiddish Proverb that says *If you don't want to do something, one excuse is as good as another.* So, I grabbed a piece of paper, a sharpie and scribbled, in my big sloppy hand writing, what's your excuse. It was not pretty but it was a good question.

I was going to have a major image problem in a couple of months, and I wanted to be prepared. What would I tell people when they asked about the trip? I left the note on the dining room table so I would see it as I passed to my office, and I would see it as I passed to the fridge, and I would see it when I was dodging the work that needed done. The note scoffed at me, and it taunted me for a couple of hours.

Finally, I picked up the phone. If you have ever dreaded making phone calls for any reason you will sympathize when I say the receiver weighed at least one hundred pounds as I held it to my ear. Still, I swallowed my excuses and called five customers because that was a goal I could handle. Just five people, the easy ones I was sure would say "NO" so I could go back to avoiding what I needed to do. Well, you can probably guess what happened, I scheduled an event, and I sold some product.

Feeling brave, I asked a fellow consultant if she still wanted to try to earn the cruise. She did, and she was on track with more points than me. For some reason, she accepted me as a pacing partner anyway. Feeling encouraged, I sold some more product. Strangely, the phone no longer weighed a hundred pounds; I could call people I thought would say "Yes!" I even recruited someone simply by offering her the opportunity to join my team. Apparently, she hadn't heard I'd been a loser lately.

I did all the things I had been avoiding and, of course, none of it was as hard as I had made it seem during the last couple of months. Isn't that the way it always is when you procrastinate? The things you avoid are seldom as big as the time and effort you use in avoiding them.

I always tried to be off the phone to have time to visit with my teenager when she came home from school. It is what we should do as parents, take time to listen to our kids. Take time to say your day is important to me, and I want to hear about it. Take time to give feedback and time to be, well, a parent. There's seldom an excuse to answer the phone when you are talking to your child. There's seldom a reason to say, "hold on" when they are about to tell you about history class.

There is, however, our responsibility to teach children how to be strong, productive adults. People who contribute to the world are seldom raised by people who don't contribute to the world. I stopped, listened to her stories from the day, and I went back to work.

After a while, I realized she had not been around for quite some time. I started wondering what was going on. No loud music. No snacking. No asking for a friend to come over. I believe both teens and puppies are like two- year -olds; if they are quiet I start to worry and an investigation is usually needed.

I hung up the phone and went to check on things. You won't believe what I discovered. There was my teen busily working on a project I had been nagging about for several weeks. Being the ever-effective parent I had asked, reasoned, cajoled, bribed and, like all good parents, been ignored. I'd not given up…. But I guess I had given in.

I said "Wow- what are you doing?" "Organizing my closet." I said, "Why today?" and she said, "Because you left that note on the table." I replied with something parental like "carry on" or "good job" and went to see just what magical note I had left on the table.

The only thing on the table was my "what's your excuse" note. A light bulb went off. She thought it was for her! I didn't see the need to dispel her of this conclusion.

I went back to work and was on the phone when my husband came home. Now, because I was self-employed and worked from home I had decided I needed to hug him when he came in. I also *needed* to listen to stories from his day, prepare dinner, watch Jeopardy, do just about everything a 1960s-domestic goddess would do except wear a shirtwaist and throw cocktail parties. He didn't expect it but it made for a handy way to derail my goals.

On that day, something was different. On that day, I was clicking along, I could tell after one day of truly focused work that I was on to something; if I made the calls, sold the product, and scheduled the events I just might have a business. Who knew? I realized, after one day of true focus, I truly could and would achieve that trip!

Knowing he supported me 100%, and that he fully expected to be on that cruise I waved hello to my husband, dialed the phone and went back into conversation. After about 30 minutes I wondered where he was and why the theme from Jeopardy was not playing, like the background music of my evenings, in the living room.

Again, an investigation was in order. I discovered Jeopardy was not on because my dear husband was patching a hole that had been in the driveway for about three years. A hole I learned to ignore so I didn't have to nag.

I slipped on my snow boots, threw on a coat and headed out the door to applaud and, yes, to investigate why today was the big day. I determined it would be wise to approach this in a womanly sort of way, not proceed with an in your face interrogation.

While it is kind of hard to cuddle up to a man wearing a parka, who has a shovel in one hand and a bag of pavement patch in the other, I did the best I could and whispered in his ear, "Whatcha doin'?"

His reply was simply this. "Well, you left that note on the table."

Insert laughter here.

And, if nagging and ignoring have not done the trick at your house allow yourself time to write a sign for your dining room table. You never know who might think it is for them and with any luck the odd jobs will get done, and you will earn a trip.

Does that story sound familiar to you? Do you have a big goal you fear you have let slide away? Do you have a goal are you going to have to admit publicly you are not achieving? What goal can people simply see you are not achieving? Is there an unmet goal bugging you right now?

Grab a fresh sheet of paper and write your goal near the top. (I've inserted a sheet so you can do it in this book if a paper is not close at hand.)

Now be honest with yourself. Be honest with me. Pretend you are looking at a note on the table and answer this question. What's your excuse? What is the crippling excuse that is holding you back from achieving your goal? Is it health, sloth, or knowledge? Is it time, distraction or any other of a myriad of excuses? What do you say to your loved ones? What do you tell your boss?

What's your excuse?

Take a deep breath. About half way down your sheet of paper write down your excuse for failure.

I have done this exercise with hundreds of people, so I assure you I know that when people read the words "write it down" they don't. They just flip the page. Please don't, we are on a journey to your goal. Just write down your big goal and your excuse for failure.

Now you can flip the page.

What's Your Excuse?

My Goal:

My Excuse(s) for failure:

Here is a printable sign just in case you need it.

What's

Your

Excuse?

What's Your Excuse?

Chapter 3

THIS and THAT

You are now holding a piece of paper that says a lot about you; your goal followed by your excuse. You have a choice. Your choice is to be like Tony, holding on to that excuse for dear life, never changing your pattern, never achieving your goal. Or you can take that excuse and ask yourself this question: Will it hold up? Is it worth the breath it will take to say your excuse? Are you proud of it?

If not, scribble it out. Scribble and deface your excuse. Tear it to shreds. Throw it on the floor or burn it in a candle. I want you to make a mess of the excuse that has made a mess of you. If there is more than one excuse for your failure, write them down and mess them up too.

Excuses can stall the great moments of your life. Take a deep breath and hear yourself and the excuses you give. What have you said that limits your experiences? What have you missed out on because of your excuses? I often hear people say, "I'm too fat." "I don't have a degree." "I never learned to manage money."

All are excuses to stay on the couch watching actors and reality stars instead of getting out and participating in fulfilling activities or vying for a promotion. Is that what you really want?

In my house we love adventure, and we love to try the next thing. I have a friend, Patty, who is overweight. Being overweight causes her to say, "I don't want to participate" when she actually does. While a group of us were preparing to white water raft in Denali National Park, Patty said she wasn't going. Her excuses? "I might get cold." "I don't like to get my face wet." "I don't know how to paddle."

While these are all valid reasons for staying on the shore Patty confessed this to me, "I don't think there will be a dry suit in my size." Patty wanted to go; she just did not want to be embarrassed. I asked her to remain open to the adventure, if there was a suit in her size I'd help her put it on, and she could join us. If there wasn't one I'd buy her some coffee and she could stay warm in the launch cabin with a good book and the company of young, handsome river guides. She agreed.

Now, no tourist adventure company would say "no" to a paying client if the activity is safe, so of course they had a suit in her size. She wiggled into it much easier than expected, but because she is also short the long, rubberized legs, bunched up and turned her walk into a comical waddle. Patty laughed and paraded around in great spirit. Climbing into the raft was a fast slide as her rubber suit hit the frost covered gunnel. Patty lay in the bottom of the raft, unable to right herself, laughing her infectious laughter, which made everyone else laugh too.

Some people would have said "I'm done" if they looked like an orange turtle upside down in the bottom of a boat, but the goal was rafting and the excuse of a non-fitting suit had been negated. Patty was going! Three people helped her up, and we took off down the river.

We all screamed.

We all laughed.

We all experienced the thrill of white water in our faces on a day when the temperature was only thirty-nine degrees. We were bumping and thumping off rocks and paddling like crazy when the guide yelled "left" or "right."

Not one person had a bigger smile than Patty. She even leaned into the spray of the water as it cascaded over us.

Patty had let go of excuses, shared an adventure, proved to herself she was capable and in the process earned a great memory. She almost missed it though, and I have a feeling you have missed some fun memories because of excuses. Go ahead and list them now.

I've missed:

Do you look at that list of things you have missed and see it is just not worth it? Do you lie awake at night thinking of what you aren't doing? Do you waste energy thinking of who you will have to admit your failure to before much longer? Do you let your excuses stymie your goals and your adventures? Do you waste time and energy thinking you are not good enough?

Does it feel ridiculous?

It is completely ridiculous you know.

You have a goal and you have a life to live. Excuses should not limit you. Look at your goal. Really look at it, internalize everything it means to you. This is a goal that could define you. A goal you have carried around but not achieved. So, let me ask you a question, can you do it? If your answer to that question was "Yes!" then I have a bigger, more important question.

Will you do it?

Right there, that intake of breath when I asked will you do it; that was your moment of truth.

Did you sigh and say "No?" or did you take in the breath, let it out with confidence and a puffed chest and say "YES! I want to achieve this goal."? If you said "YES!" skip right to the next chapter- you have the right goal. If you said "no" stick with me for a minute.

I like to play THIS and THAT with goals. If you want this, you must do that. It's surprisingly effective and has saved me and others from setting a lot of goals we really didn't want. I'll give you an example.

I have several friends who are marathoners. They look great; they have wonderful stories and a passion for running 26.2 miles that is simply infectious. Under the influence of their inspiration, I set *the* goal to run with them. I even told a room full of several hundred women my goal, "I am going to run a marathon."

Now, I am built for comfort, not speed so this was quite an ambitious goal. I was in great shape at the time, and I set out running every other day. I ran for several weeks and knew my THIS- running the marathon, was a fun goal. Then I found out that to be well trained, with the program we were following, I had to run for six hours straight the two Saturday's before the marathon.

The THAT of running, bored to tears, devoting six unbroken hours of my time to running on a Saturday was simply not worth it to me, running an hour took every ounce of mental energy I could muster. Sure, I felt the runner's high- but I was still bored. So, I unset the goal and returned to exercise that filled my soul. I'm not in marathoner shape, but last Saturday morning I sat and visited with friends instead of running for six hours. To me it was worth giving up that goal and I learned a lot about myself.

Playing THIS and THAT works for just about every goal. If the THIS is to climb Mt. Everest, the THAT is packing your feces up and down the mountain. (I know- YUCK- but it's true!) If the THIS is opening a new store, the THAT is often sixteen hour days for little or no pay for several years. If the THIS is a new baby, the THAT is 2a.m. feedings. (Totally worth it!) If the THIS is a whole new look, the THAT is cutting your hair. If the THIS is retiring rich, the THAT may be giving up mocha's and living on a budget. If the THIS is learning to surf, the THAT is swimming past the breakers.

THIS is the goal; it is what you declare you are working towards. THAT is the hardest, most frustrating part of achieving your goal. To play THIS and THAT you simply compare the two to see which wins. If the THIS (goal) is bigger and considerably more gratifying than the THAT (hardest task) you win. You have a goal you will achieve. If the THAT is so distasteful you don't think you can work through it, the THIS is probably never going to happen. Try it out on your goal.

THIS: (your goal)

THAT: (hardest part of achieving your goal)

If you want THIS you must do THAT is a pretty simple concept, but I hope you can see the power of thinking through the good the bad and the ugly as you set your goal. If you are thinking "Well, good grief, anyone can carry their feces," then climbing a mountain could be your goal. If you say, "Six hours of running sounds like a dream come true," then maybe you should run a marathon. However, if the THAT, the worst part of your goal is undoable in your mind you have the wrong goal.

I am sorry to have to say that to you. Sometimes the hardest thing to hear is simply "that is not your goal." Instead, that goal is probably something you feel you should do, or something you "have to do." Truth be told, it is something you just aren't going to do because it is the wrong goal.

If you can't imagine yourself making those sales, running that race, earning that trip, starting that business, if you aren't willing to move a mountain to get that goal simply let it go and look forward. This means you will have to get over it.

I know, 'get over it' sounds rather cold and abrupt. I don't like to appear blunt, but I am certain life is too short to lament a goal you really don't want. So, with my permission and loving suggestion, get over it.

As you get over it, you can set a better goal, it will be okay. Let it go.

I am letting go of the goal to:

Doesn't that feel better? Just writing it down (you did write it down, didn't you?) can be freeing. The things we carry in our heads often look silly on paper. I once wrote down that I was letting go of the goal to have clean windows April first. It had been such a chore and bother, especially if there was a late season storm, yet I'd worry and fuss if they weren't sparkly by the last weekend in March. Then I wrote down 'I am letting go of clean windows April first' and let it go. I also laughed when I saw it in writing because no-one else cared if my windows sparkled April first or June twelfth. I felt guilt for something that was big in my head but trivial on paper.

Write down what you are letting go of, laugh a bit, and move on. Your right goal is waiting.

What's Your Excuse?

Chapter 4

Declaring Your Goal

You are now ready for YOUR goal so let's talk about how to declare what you really want so you can achieve it. This means knowing it is your goal, not your mom's goal, not your boss's goal or your spouse's goal. Your goal should be your goal.

While Patty had a great time rafting, I've always wondered if she put on that suit to help me achieve my goal- a group of people I enjoyed all living an adventure in Denali- or was it truly her goal to conquer those rapids. I know she does not regret going, but it was probably not a defining goal for her.

A defining goal should be something that comes from your heart. Something that makes you breathe a bit deeper. Something that makes you more you and probably scares you just a little. Something that you know you can achieve no matter how bad it might get in the process. It might even be something that changes your life completely.

In a few pages, I am going to ask you to declare that goal. It will be your goal, not a goal you are supposed to have or a goal with a THAT you can't imagine doing. You are going to choose a goal that will define you.

After achieving this goal, you will be able to say to yourself and others "I am (insert descriptor like an author, a mountain climber, a dancer, a marathoner, a master chef.)" and you will smile from the inside when you say it.

Remember when I said I wasn't a goal setter? I was once so scared of life that I cried if I had to talk to more than about three people at once. Could it have had something to do with the fact the first time I gave a speech in high school English, I chose a serious heartfelt subject but the opening sentence made my classmates roar with laughter and subsequently tease me to this day? Probably.

I wallowed in that story for years until I was elected, mostly because I was not brave enough to say no to the nomination, PTA president. I was not scared. I was petrified. I am not prone to panic attacks, but I wished I was; I wanted to curl up and just avoid the whole thing. I simply could not speak to a large group with the skills I possessed at the time.

After my overreaction and a bit of soul searching, I declared my goal to speak in public. I knew with the support of some good people and a little bit of 'to hell with it' in my belly that I *was* going to talk to those parents in the school gym. After all, they were just people sitting on folding chairs with gum wads under the seats, and they didn't want to do a speech either.

As a young housewife living in Rapid City, South Dakota, with clothes from a thrift store and hair that needed cut, I joined Toastmasters International. I cried and shook so hard during my first speech that two men in three-piece business suits came to the podium, standing on either side of me as I melted down.

They both placed a hand on my back (to hold me up I imagine!) and got me through that speech. They did the same thing for my second speech a couple of weeks later. By the third speech I stood alone, still scared but knowing they supported me.

To this day, when I give a speech I feel the warmth of those hands. Men whose names I don't even recall gave me strength I still draw on when I talk from a stage. The speech can be off the cuff, or off the TelePrompTer, and unlike when I was in ninth grade English, I now think the more laughter and tears in the audience the better. I can give a speech and entertain an audience, all because I declared my goal to be a public speaker.

What I hope you hear in my story of public speaking is that you are worthy. People will support you, even people you don't know very well. It does not matter if you are, like I was, not quite polished. You are capable of more and achieving your goal matters. Perhaps you *are* polished and you want to see what it feels like to get your hands dirty playing in the mud of your own garden.

Do it.

You are designed to fill your wildest dreams, live your best life, and smile every day. What is the worst that can happen? I learned to give a speech. You might learn to grow a tomato. It's going to be your goal; I and so many others want you to achieve it.

Now that I have warmed you up, it is your turn to declare your goal. This will be a defining goal, a goal that you will be proud to achieve. What goal scares you just a bit or fills you with wonder? What goal is worth every THAT you can think of? Is it to lose 30 pounds? Is it to write a book? Sail an ocean? Earn a trip? Improve your grades? Make some sales? Run a race? Be a PTA president? Grow a tomato?

It does not have to be gigantic; but it does have to be something you can control. Something you want to do, something you are willing to work to achieve. If you have not heard before now, winning the lottery is not a goal, it is a dream. And probably more correctly should be considered a complete surprise. Think about your goal again. Is it truly a goal? Is it truly your goal? If you are sure, if you are ready, willing, and able to achieve this goal, declare it by writing it down.

My right goal is to:

Look how wonderful that looks! Your goal is proudly
declared in your handwriting. Simply writing down
your goal moves you so much closer to achieving it that
you probably should start preparing for your victory
party now. To make sure that victory party takes place,
there are a couple of more steps you should take to
ensure you are ready for this to be your working goal.

What's Your Excuse?

Chapter 5

Validate Your Goal

You have thought through your goal and declared it, now you are going to begin the work of making it even more concrete in your mind and thus more achievable. When you decide to make something happen you need to understand why. This means asking yourself what exactly this goal means to you.

When validating your goal with your WHY you want to think of everything that this goal means to you. What will change in your appearance, your outlook, or your family? Will achieving your goal have a financial impact? Will it save your job, help others, or improve your health? Will you be able to tell your mother- in - law "Ha! I did it?!" (Disclaimer- I have a great mother-in- law, but I've heard some of them are a tad hard to deal with.) Will it just be fun, introduce you to new cultures or allow you to learn a new skill? Why do these things matter to you?

In 2010 I quit a long term career I loved and sat, morose, on the patio for about a day. I was fully prepared to mope about for a week or so, but as often happens when you think you'll have nothing to do for a few days, a project pops up. My project was Operation Feed the Swedes.

No, I did not start a charity for underprivileged Swedish families; the Swedes in this case were two young men,

Edvin and Emil, who were bicycling across America. My husband and I saw them in a nearby park and invited them to pitch a tent in our back yard for the night.

Because we have a house full of people at all times, and love to entertain, the guests fit right in and decided to spend the upcoming Fourth of July weekend with us. Six days later, when we said goodbye, I had a new appreciation for goal setting and they had seen their first parade, first fireworks, and had taken a nice hike in the Beartooth Mountains. They had also eaten every American food we could think of and introduced us to caviar and eggs for breakfast. It was a wonderful experience, one we all treasure.   (Be brave, invite a stranger to dinner!)

When first contemplating this trip, Edvin and Emil were warned not to come to America. The perception their family and friends had of us was not flattering. Apparently, we sit on the front porch with our shirts on, holding guns, and possess a Clint Eastwood, Dirty Hairy attitude.

They also were told America has more than our fair share of lunatics and live in constant fear with no respect for personal boundaries. The fact that their first night in America included a sexual advance so disturbing they sneaked out of their host's home at two a.m. really did nothing to dissolve those perceptions.

The big question then is why. Why did they fly from the comfort of home to risk harm, eat peanut butter for almost every meal, sleep in roadside ditches and walk with a bit of biker's limp, caused by days on end of hills and prairies? They did not even own bikes before this trip so biking wasn't 'in their nature.' What would make them take on this goal?

When I asked Edvin that question, he laughed and said "Well, I am 21."

While that might explain why they were tougher than any hill, the riders did have a great list of reasons. They wanted to see the Rockies and other scenery. They wanted to meet the *nice* people in America. They wanted to say they had done it. They wanted to experience a summer of doing what they wanted, when they wanted, a new culture, and hopefully meet a few nice American girls. They had a list of foods they wanted to try, places they wanted to see and the goal to prove they could ride from sea to shining sea.

A few days after leaving here the guys sent us a picture; Edvin was hugging a downhill sign as if it was his long-lost brother. He said he'd never been so happy to see the top of a hill in his life, as it seemed they had ridden uphill the entire morning. In that goofy, hanging on for dear life, moment you could see his smile and almost hear their laughter.

They had conquered another goal, a mountain pass. There would be others, but they were on their way to the sea and a delicious crab dinner with friends in Seattle. Life was good.

Because they took time to develop a list of WHY'S to conquer their goal, nothing slowed them down. They had quickly figured out American's are very welcoming, especially in small towns, and they spent more nights in guest rooms than their small tent. They worked on a horse ranch in South Dakota for two weeks, saw some of Canada, avoided riding through our biggest cities, embraced our smallest towns and learned about our native cultures. Their muscles adapted to the task and their system of packing, riding, unpacking, became second nature.

WHY'S kept Edvin and Emil pedaling forward, always knowing the goal was in front of them, and that they were doing something truly defining. They were stronger men because of this goal, and they would have stories to tell for years to come.

Your WHY list may include things that are both personal, and sharable with anyone who asks. The point is to make a complete list of the things that matter to you. You may want to include things such as: personal satisfaction, health, income, or "for the challenge." Your list should go on and on with every reason you can think to add.
Would you become famous, help animals, or simply see what it feels like to cross a finish line? Write them down. Think big. Think small. Just think about all the reasons you want to achieve the goal you have declared.

List your reasons WHY here:

Why should you write them down? Because the more reasons you must achieve this goal the fewer excuses you can have to avoid this goal. The longer your list of reasons, the bigger your chance of success becomes. Holding the list in your head does not work when life gets in the way and your spirit is weak. Having a carefully thought out list to hold in your hands will make the difference between giving in and giving it your all. If you are going to bike up the Rockies, you want to know a crab dinner and soft bed are waiting on the other side.

Do you have enough WHYS on your list? Are your WHYS big enough to overcome doubt and propel you past failure? Does your goal feel a little more concrete? Imagine how you will feel when you achieve your goal; who will you tell first? How will you celebrate?

When I achieve my goal, I will:

It is exciting to see this goal coming together. You declared what you want, and you have validated why you want it. Now it is time to dig in and establish how you are going to make your goal something you actually achieve.

What's Your Excuse?

Chapter 6

Be a Goal Getter

My grandmother said "Some people are like blisters. They only show up when all the work is done." My family helped me to establish a strong work ethic; I never wanted to be a blister. My first real job was at the drive-in at the Flintstones Theme Park. Pretty exciting stuff, huh? Still, I learned so much about work there, especially from my boss, Glenn, who always said "If you have time to lean, you have time to clean." While I didn't always find joy in cleaning the ice cream machines, those two sayings helped me to appreciate the value of the good hard work which is needed to be a goal getter.

Sadly, I have seen people who call themselves goal setters be just that, goal *setters*. They set a goal but they never dig in and go to work so they can be a goal *getter*. Anyone can be a goal setter. I set the goal to run a marathon, but I didn't achieve it. Achieving a goal takes someone willing to roll up their sleeves and do whatever it actually takes.

My most fervent wish for you is that this book will in some way help you to feel the satisfaction of being a goal achiever. It is a great feeling and you deserve it.

Part of the disconnect between setting and achieving goals is not clearly understanding everything it will take to accomplish the goal. In this step, you are going to make a list of all the work your goal requires. You are going to look for any THATS which could derail you and hopefully you will find that you are already part way to reaching your goal.

So that you can see how this comes together, let's use the steps I learned while working toward my goal of finishing this book.

Goal: Finishing *What's Your Excuse*

WHY: I'm ready. People are waiting for it. If I don't finish it, I can't start the next thing. I want to say, "I am an author." I want to help other people with a few stories and a shot of 'can do' for their goals. If I can do this, so can my friends who want to write a book; I want to be able to mentor them with experience. Etc. (Sorry, you don't get to Etc. your list- It's called author privilege.)

HOW: Spend at least two hours per day for the next week in edit mode. Swallow my pride and ask for help. Print, circle, type, read, think, talk, forget about doing dishes, ask, reread, retype, evaluate, cut, add and think some more. Accept criticism. Accept praise. Set it aside for one week and re-evaluate. (There is more, but you get the idea.)

My **THIS** is having a finished book. My **THAT** is definitely the 'pain' of being tied to a desk.

Now that you have had a look at a working example of the goal setting steps in action it is time to work on your HOW list. The overarching question you should ask yourself is 'what do I need to do to achieve my goal?' You won't want to skimp on this list, and you should include the wonderful things like taking in the scenery you will view while riding from sea to sea and the painful things like blister pads or eating broccoli.

If you don't know all the steps required to achieve your goal, look them up or talk to someone who has achieved a similar goal. Listing and understanding every step is more important than generally imagined.

Often, when working on their list, the people I have coached find they've already done much of the work required to achieve their goal. It seems they knew what they wanted and subconsciously worked towards it; they just had not put everything together and evaluated it before. I hope this happens for you.

The other thing you may discover is that there is a step on your HOW list which you have been skipping all along and it becomes obvious that working diligently on that one activity will make all the difference. This can be a happy discovery, one missing link in the chain of goal evolution, which explains everything.

Here are a few ideas to get you going on your HOW list:

Do you need to learn something? What and from whom?

Do you need to go somewhere? Where and when?

Do you need to exercise? How much and when?

How many sales would you need to make? How many cold calls will that take? How much time will you need to devote to follow up? Who is the best person to start with?

Do you need to eat right? Well, what exactly does right mean? Write down what you are a going to eat, and when.

Are you writing a cookbook? How many recipes will you develop and test? When?

Do you need to call people? Who? When? How often?

Do you need money? How much and what can you do to get that money? Legally, of course. (No, I did not say earn, not all money is earned but that is another subject.)

Think about your relationships for a moment. Who do you need to ask for help and who do you need to ask to get out of your way?

Sometimes that is the hardest part, telling others how they can help you, or worse, how they hinder you. If your WHY is right and big enough these conversations flow easily, and I am willing to bet that in 9 out of 10 conversations the other person wants what is best for you anyway!

Of course, some lists are longer than others, so just make your HOW list as big as you need. Be honest with yourself. Try not to skip steps and try to establish firm times and dates for as much of the work as possible. If you want to be more spiritual, write down what time of the day you will practice your faith so you can stick to it. If you need to build something, write down any tools you will need to purchase and how much you expect to pay for them. Details make a difference.

The point of this list is not to overwhelm you. It is to liberate your goal. The best list will make your goal doable in a sequential and orderly fashion. If you don't know every step, every THAT, every benefit and every detail you will have some surprises along the way. If you are the type of person who is okay with unknowns popping up, just list the big things. If you don't like surprises, be more thorough.

My HOW List:

HOW is not all about drudgery and boredom, so I hope you have a few things on your list you are excited about. It can be about the fun things you will see and learn as you prepare to be an achiever. I had a goal to truly see and experience New York City for an anniversary a few years ago.

When I wrote on my how list 'reserve hotel for ten nights' I about did a back flip. I'd not really thought about ten nights of city lights until that moment, and it made the work of getting everything in line for that trip pleasant to think about.

A complete HOW list really helps you to know your goal. Because you are working on your defining goal, and I am going to ask you the big question in a few pages, you might want to walk around the block; think about your HOWS and make sure you are satisfied with your list before we choose a goal due date.

What's Your Excuse?

Chapter 7

Declare a Due Date

Today I was hiking a beautiful mountain trail. Breath, when I could catch it, was cold and ragged. Two women jogged by me- and they had the nerve to be talking normally. I joked to myself that they were rather thoughtless flaunting their health and having a great time while I took twice as long as them to reach the same vista point. In seriousness though, I knew the THIS of easy breath and the THAT of jogging this trail regularly were not my goal, it was theirs.

Since the trail was not in my home town, and I've already gone through the whole running thing, I stopped and listened to the wind through the grass, I felt the chill on my cheeks, and I took in the glory of evening sunlight on mountain snow. Life felt pretty good. I did not have to run up the mountain; I could enjoy the hike at my speed.

While standing in satisfaction and peaceful surroundings I realized I did have a defining goal to finish this book which was coming due soon. I turned around, content with the experience, and returned to the goal I truly wanted to achieve. This reflection exercise was liberating, not limiting.

I knew what I wanted and didn't have to chase after the new goal of trail jogging, even though it would be satisfying. You will be able to use your well-planned goal and due date in exactly the same way. It is kind of a gut check tool and you will find yourself saying 'I *want this* shiny goal, which just caught my attention, but I truly WANT this great big defining goal!'

As you can see from that example, having a date chosen for the completion of your goal is incredibly important. Having a vague date of "sometime" will not keep you on task. When establishing your goal's due date, you need to be realistic. How often can you work on your goal? How will you adapt to "life" when events happen that affect your timetable? Are there outside pressures like an incentive period or milestone event?

You will want to take a good hard look at your defining goal, and the why you have established for accomplishing your goal, and compare those to the time allotted for all the tasks on your how list. Do they mesh with the due date? Are you being too easy on yourself? Are you being too hard on yourself? At this point, you need to massage the date, or the other parameters of the goal to make certain it fits you and your current lifestyle.

It is not a bad idea to make a chart, breaking your goal into smaller doable chunks so you have way points along your path. Those way points allow for time to check in and make certain you are on track to your goal. If you have a year to achieve your goal, this means you should have a big check in at the six month point and half of your task list should be accomplished. Three months from today you should have one quarter of your goal achieved. Monthly and weekly goals can be broken down from there.

Let's say your goal is to take the kids to Disney Land. You want to do it next winter, and you are budgeting $3000 for the trip. This is what your check in points may look like:

Goal- save $3000 for a trip to Disney Land

Month	January	March	June	September	December
Money saved	$250	$750	$1500	$2250	$3000

From this goal of $3000 in twelve months you know that $250 a month is what you will need to save. $250 per month breaks down to approximately $58 per week or $8.30 per day. You know can decide how you will save or earn an extra $8.30 per day for this trip, your defining goal.

Breaking it down to this granular level makes the goal achievable and you can make decisions about small purchases each day knowing how they impact your big goal.

At each of the way points you set for your goal be honest with yourself and ask questions such as: Are you doing the work? Are you on target? What needs to change?

Many people use a good old-fashioned calendar for this type of planning. It is easy to record what you need to do in the given time period and easy to see exactly what your goal looks like when compared against the march of time.

When working with the calendar or chart you should not only detail your way points, but also mark out holidays, vacations, family events, and other pertinent information so you know what challenges and rewards you will have along the way. The more effort you put into the date, the more likely you are to be able to actually meet the date you have set.

With your chart, calendar, or milestone in mind it's time to declare when you will achieve your goal. Will it be Thursday? Will it be December 31st? Maybe by your birthday? What date will you be able to say mission accomplished?

I will achieve my goal on or before:

You have declared your goal, validated your why, established each step in your how list and now you have a reasonable date for accomplishment. The opportunity to call yourself a goal achiever, not just a goal setter is coming together nicely now. As we move forward from here you are going to take one more big step, followed by establishing your excuse for success.

What's Your Excuse?

Chapter 8

The Big Question

Let's look at where you have been. You have defined your goal, established a WHY, written out your HOW list and your due date is ready and waiting. Four big steps have clarified what you want and probably helped you to see yourself a bit more clearly. If you are like me and that marathon goal you got part way through the steps and said "Nope, this is too much work. I am not working for that goal!" and then you started over.

I can't tell you how important and how okay that act of starting over is! You will want to massage your goal, sleep on your decision, and evaluate the work involved as well as the consequences and the rewards of achieving your goal. When your goal makes it through the process it is the right goal.

What makes it the right goal is your conscious decision to examine it and say "Yes! Like a precious treasure I am going to hold this goal in my hands and give it everything it deserves -- my time, my talent, and my devotion." You now have a goal you can be proud to pursue.

Knowing that you will achieve the goal you hold in your
hands, your head, and your heart takes one final step.
It takes the big question and if I were your goal I'd be
down on one knee with tears in my eyes when I ask
you this question, it is that important.

When you say "Yes!" to this final question it means you
will develop the focus, drop any excuses for failure and
achieve this goal. It means you are ready, that you
agree to every step, and you understand every benefit.
You are saying yes you have pride in the goal you have
set and you can imagine yourself as a goal achiever.
So, here it is; the big question.

Will you do it?

Did you take a big breath when I asked, "Will you do
it?" In your heart, you already know what it means.
Did that breath say, "Hot dog and hallelujah let's go!?"
Or, did you sigh because it is all just too much work?
Did you sigh because you just can't fathom achieving
this goal? Or did you exhale with excitement to get
started? Are you committed or are you unsure?

Any one of these answers is the right answer. You
must know what you want and what you are willing to
do for a defining goal. You have read in this book how I
let go of wrong goals and how I latched on to right
goals and you have seen others do the same. You can
do it too. So, if you sighed "no," start again. Adjust the
goal, validate it with a bigger why, or choose a different
due date.

Change the parameters until it is your right goal or
scribble it out and get going with another goal.

When your goal is right you are going to sit a little straighter. You will be proud to tell loved ones about your plans. You are going to smile from the inside and you are going to achieve the goal. You may even begin working towards it right now, you feel that committed.

Here's the thing. If you have really worked the steps, if you have played THIS and THAT, if you have looked at your goal from the bottom and the top, from beginning to end and you still want that goal, it is your right goal.

Achieving your right goal is going to feel amazing!

You won't care if anyone else cheers for you because you are going to cheer for yourself. Sure, life will come at you in crazy ways. Kids will get sick. Dogs will get run over. The sun will come out and friends will call. Cake will be served for dessert and you just might lose your job.

This time when challenges like those arise it will be okay. You can get past them now that you have said "Yes!" and the goal is truly the goal *you* want and understand. To help you break through any roadblocks you are going to want an excuse for success, it will make all of the difference as you travel along to your goal.

What's Your Excuse?

Chapter 9

The Right Excuse

I am so proud of you for taking the steps to set a goal you can truly achieve. Sometimes it can be a lot of work to think through everything and to write it all down, but in doing so you should be feeling more confident and content that you will make your goal happen this time. You fully understand it now.

You will find as you work this system of goal setting it will become easier and you can almost short cut through because you begin to know yourself and you learn what your hang ups can be. That is what we are going to talk about in this chapter. Recognizing that some days it will feel easier to just give in and give up but knowing in your heart that is not the right plan.

We begin by thinking about your goal again, knowing the work it will take to achieve your goal and the reasons you want your goal. You have committed to them but you could make one excuse after the other to not achieve your goal. You may have done it before and you may do it again; set a goal, get distracted, and lose enthusiasm. Unless you have the right excuse.

What exactly is the right excuse? The right excuse is your excuse for success, it is your reason for getting out of bed and climbing over the roadblocks. It is what you keep close to your heart and pull out when the going gets tough. No-one else may ever know your excuse for success. The fact that you know it is enough.

Some would say they are 'reasons' for success but I would argue that if we are hardwired and well-practiced at giving excuses why not just develop the right excuse? Use a little creative dissonance to help your brain move in the direction you truly want to go.

Remember my cruise? The one I publicly announced I would achieve then sat back and did nothing to actually earn. I'm proud to tell you my pacing partner and I both earned the trip. My husband was not swimming behind the ship looking for another consultant. Paul was walking by my side as we were first to board the ship, privileged to be greeted by the captain and leaders of our company.

Actually, I was the 5th highest point earner for this particular trip. I had let go of failure excuses, worked like crazy and made sure everyone knew what I was doing. I quickly built excitement into my business and my customers fed off that enthusiasm and helped me achieve my goal. People like to be around success and they like it even more if they can contribute to success.

In Billings, Montana, where I currently live, we have a star realtor. He has a distinctive look, an incredible work ethic and a gift with people. What I enjoy most is hearing people say "I bought my house from him" in hushed tones. It is almost as if they are in awe of his greatness and quietly bragging that they helped him to climb to the top, which of course they did.

What's Your Excuse?

On the cruise, being a top achiever meant I enjoyed first class service, a suite with two Jacuzzi's and a private butler, Elvis. (No kidding, he really was named Elvis.) As was true of all top point earners I was generally treated like I knew what I was doing.

People asked what I had done to earn so many points and I was happy to share the secrets of success. I skipped the part containing all of the excuses. Some things are better left untold when you are basking in the glory of a goal achieved.

I told them about making sure everyone knew my goal. I also explained the strategy of being ready with a list of ways customers could help me reach my goal if they offered to support me. This is a step you may want to adopt. To achieve your goal do you need money? Do you need a babysitter while you write your business plan? Do you need a pacing partner or a few tips on reaching your goal? Be ready to say so. People want to help or they wouldn't offer to help.

I suggest you think of these small requests not as a show of weakness, but as a small gift you give to other people. If you are not organized, ask someone who is to help you organize your office. If you don't possess a green thumb, ask for help from someone who does. Being able to do what they are good at while helping you to achieve your goal is good for both of you. They will feel pride and you will feel gratitude, so be ready to ask for and accept the help you need.

On the cruise, I told fellow consultants what I said on the phone to sell and schedule. Most importantly, I told them I made the excuse to be a success, not a failure.

My excuse for success was twofold. Privately I needed to prove to myself that I was capable.

Most people who met me would have been surprised to learn I didn't feel capable and I didn't really want to go into it so I also had a more public excuse. Publicly I said if I was going on the cruise I was going in style; which meant three times the work I normally did in my business.

My favorite cruise memory is the day I took an afternoon to myself. I ordered champagne and strawberries which were rolled in on a lovely cart with roses and assorted chocolates. Feeling decadent I jumped into the patio Jacuzzi and soaked away the afternoon. The sky and the water were the exact same shade of blue and as we floated along I reveled in the beauty and the peace.

At that moment, I felt complete balance; something I had not had in the mad dash to achieve this moment. I looked back at the pace I had set for several months and knew soaking in that tub, while Elvis prepared warm towels, was worth the craziness. Three times the work meant ten times the pleasure. Life is good my friends when you do what you set out to do.

That is what I counted on back in October when I scribbled the simple "what's your excuse" sign. I could either have an excuse for my failure (I'm too busy) or an excuse for my success (three times the work). I could do what I set out to do, or I could find an excuse for failure.

I figured an excuse for my success was going to be a lot more fun. So, on the cruise, strutting around like I had worked for nine months not four I was able to say, "I did three times the volume I normally do in my business" when people asked me "How?"

That is what I want you to imagine now -- imagine the day of complete success. You are at the podium giving an acceptance speech or your name is on the top spot of the sales board. Perhaps you imagine yourself being recognized for your accomplishment while standing in line at the grocery or you are leaning on a tree after the marathon. Someone approaches you and says, "How did you do it?" Or perhaps "Why did you do it?" And you get to give your best excuse ever! You get to tell them why you are enjoying success, not failure. Satisfaction of accomplishment runs through you. You are a success.

What will you tell them? You might not give your deepest most personal excuse for success, as I said, that might just be for you. Now, instead of hiding behind unmet goals and lame excuses you get to say, "I was able to do it because I ran the miles, made the calls, took the classes..." Whatever your excuse for success is, imagine how good that excuse will feel as it rolls off your tongue!

This is new territory. Instead of giving an excuse for failure, the type of excuse you've grown comfortable giving, you get to be a role model. You get to be the one who achieved the goal and leads the way. It is not a mantle to be worn lightly. When you share your excuse for success you may help others imagine the same feeling of satisfaction. You may help them to know victory and confident smiles, the type of smiles that come from deep inside when you are on top of the world. The type of smile you will be wearing.

What is your excuse going to be? What will bring you success? What will get you on the phone, around the track, or to put down your second brownie? What excuse is going to drive you? What excuse will the listener respect? Will you say you did it to honor a loved one? Did you meet your goal to improve health and well-being? Is your excuse that you were trying to build a better world?   Did you just relish the adventure?   Was it just your job so you simply did it to the absolute best of your ability?

Think about your defining goal, your WHYS, your HOWS, and the date you have declared, choose your excuse for success. Write it down now so you know it when the going gets tough.

What's your private excuse for success?

What's your public excuse for success?

I promise you that if you pick the right excuse for success, not failure, you win the battle. Nothing else matters. You get what you expect and the 'What's Your Excuse' sign on your dining room table is no longer a sign of shame. It is a sign of success. A sign of things to come. A sign of what makes you, you.

What, I ask you again, is your excuse for success? It does not have to be long, it just must be right.

My Excuse for Success!

Our brains are clicking and clacking along everyday trying to reach the destination of what we expect It really is okay to have an excuse for success. Our brains are clicking and clacking along everyday trying to reach the destination of what we expect; to achieve what we practice over and over in our heads. Our brains naturally design the world we speak to and see in our thoughts. You have probably seen this fact or have read it in books and articles. Athletes visualize winning the competition, artists imagine signing the finished piece, and authors often begin with the last sentence. Your brain and your life go directly where you send them, so send them where you want to go.

The question then becomes why do we make excuses? The simple fact is they are protection. If we have a ready excuse for failure we don't have to change. We don't have to achieve. We don't have to take a good hard look at our life and admit if it is not perfect.

Now, turn that around. If we choose an excuse for success, it too is protection. It protects our best interests and tells our brains we know where we are going. And our brains just follow right along. You are capable. You have value. You can set a goal. And you can stop saying things like "It was too hard to achieve." "My boss is a jerk." "The dog ate it." You can be a goal achiever. I know you can.

If you are in a spot where you just don't believe me, where life is hard and achieving seems impossible, I want you to take a deep breath and know I have been there too. With that deep breath know that you have power and you have value.

Trust me when I say just start, take a few simple steps towards your goal and tell yourself over and over that you can do it. Just one small act of moving forward will have the effect of building momentum. "I can do it." Take a step. "I can do it." Take the next step. "I can do it." And soon you are doing it; you are achieving your goals.

Your brain believes what you tell it.

- Set a goal you want to achieve.

- Set the right excuse, the excuse that will get the job done.

- Believe in your goal. Ask for help. Ask for accountability. Do the work.

- Play your excuse for success over and over.

- Know that you can do it.

- Achieve the goal.

You are not in this alone and in the next chapter we will discuss how beneficial it is to have help when you are walking the path towards your goal.

I was never happier than when my pacing partner and I achieved the cruise together. We even posed for a photo in a shipboard pool with a banner signed by everyone who had helped us earn that moment. We sent the photo to our supporters with a loving note of gratitude. We could not have done it without them, but we could not have done it alone either, she had my back and I had hers. Let's talk about that next.

What's Your Excuse?

Chapter 10

Check Your Back

Remember, I think in some form each of us does a bit of selling every day so if you will indulge me in one more sales story I will show you how having someone behind you makes all the difference in achieving your goal.

You see, being in the trenches making a living as a sales person is both the most rewarding and the most daunting game you will ever play. You are always on and when you are not on you worry about how to get back on.

You don't want to be pushy (well, most of us don't) but you need to pay the bills. Walking the line between pushy and hungry requires the agility of a gymnast and you must do it while remembering names and trying not to pass gas. It is not for the faint of heart.

When I am in sales mode I tend to focus so much on the conversation, on the needs of the customer that I forget to breathe. It does not matter if I am selling a car or a story. I forget to breathe.

Super Salesman, Tony didn't breathe because he was afraid the customer would interrupt his barrage of words and say "No." I don't breathe because I am afraid I won't hear something I am told over the silent sound of oxygen in my lungs. I am so busy listening sometimes I forget to see.

This led to one of my infamous adventures, going on a drug deal with a demo car. How did I manage that? Well, I was busy selling the car, just selling the car. The young men liked green (go figure) and they wanted to take a test drive in our newest model which would be safe for the new baby in their family. I dashed in for keys, cleared the snowy windshield and let the 'buyer' drive.

Color sells. Letting them drive sells. Young kids can have money and my job was to make the customer happy. So, there I was, all matronly and smiling in the back seat as we swung that green car into the rough side of town. I thought it was a little strange to be there but we had already agreed that after a quick stop at their house to drop off a backpack we'd return to the dealership to sign the paper work.

My biggest sale had happened in a similar situation. A young lady who lived in an Alaskan village wanted the lipstick pink pick-up truck on our lot and she had cash from a summer of hard work on the slime line. (Salmon Processing is big business in Alaska.) When we went for a test drive she asked to swing by and show the pick-up to her cousins.

As we pulled up to the house I said, "honk the horn."

Her family poured out of the door with a wail of oooos and aaahhs and excited exclamations. Her aunt asked, "Is this your new truck?" When the customer excitedly said "YES!" I said, "We better get back to the dealership."

That lipstick pink truck is what I was thinking about while sitting in the back seat of the green sedan. I loved an easy sale and I was sure someone in the apartment we parked in front of was going to say, "Is that your car?" and I was going to smile all the way back to the dealership.

This time though, we never made it back to the dealership. A few blocks from an easy sale the police car tailing us spooked the young men. They jumped out of the car at the next stop light, ran like crazy, and I was the new showroom story. It seems everyone but me recognized what was going on. From the marijuana leaf displayed on one man's hat to the nervous behavior of his backpack toting friend, they saw what I didn't stop to take in.

While my teammates could not get my attention to prevent me from getting in that car they could call the police, and one of the salesmen followed me on my 'adventure,' ready to step in if needed. My excuse for getting in that car is that I am a trusting sort of soul who needed someone a bit more streetwise to have my back. My excuse for success is that when you have the right team, they never let you down.

That is exactly what you need as you move forward with your new goal. You have a WHY list, a HOW list, a date, and a commitment. You also have your excuse for success. You can clearly explain where you are going and why you are going there. All you need now is support.

Who wants you to achieve this goal? What will they do to help you? Who is protecting your best interests and calling for police back- up if you forget to breathe? It may be a family member, or it may be a co-worker or fellow business owner. Listing who you can count on and trust will help you feel more secure if you have a bad day.

My support comes from:

There are several possibilities for people to put on your list. When I earned the cruise, I had a pacing partner. As I do coaching, I find story after story of success coming from people who work with other like-minded people, pacing partners, or pacing teams. They have a common goal, they have common challenges, and they have sense enough to know that working together is easier than working alone.

When the day is tough a pacing partner will say "It's going to get easier, try again." They will not say "Oh, you poor, poor dear, you should just quit." When your results are high and you're right on track, your pacing partner will say "Hurrah, I am so glad it is working for you! Do you mind if I copy your example?"

Pacing partners work with the theory of abundance, meaning there is plenty of success to go around, too much for one person alone. I do not care what product you represent, or what goal you want to achieve, working together with a theory of abundance makes everything better. You learn from one another, you bolster one another and you cheer one another. Just as you learned in kindergarten- sharing makes everything better. When you work as a team you see things in a new light because you have many vantage points coming into play. You also have someone who sees the pot leaf when all you see is the sale.

I've seen the opposite of this attitude several times. "That success is mine, stay away!" The attitude - I won't share my ideas and I won't celebrate your success because it should be mine, all mine- is a sad and lonely attitude. This type of behavior leads to bitter goal setters with failing results. If you are currently working in a toxic environment be the bigger person. Open the lines of communication. Be the first to compliment and the first to assist. You will find that as you take a passion in protecting other people's backs they will protect yours too.

Another good person to have behind you is a leader or mentor who understands every step required to reach your goal. Ask them for advice and ask them to hold you accountable. Having accountability to a leader or mentor always works. I often offer the people I coach the opportunity to do a weekly check-in. On Monday, they email the best thing that happened during the previous week, in relation to their goal, and they tell me what they will do during this week. They identify any roadblock they might encounter. Most importantly they decide what will be their excuse for success.

The email check in works for any goal, this example is from someone who set the goal to be more organized.

Subject: Week of 2/8/2011

The best thing that happened last week was finally seeing the surface of my desk and I was only late for one appointment!

This week my goal is to remember to file not pile. I want to see my desk top every night when I leave the office.

My roadblock will be interruptions and appointments, I have a busy schedule and it is easy to just drop things instead of putting them away.

My excuse for success is I am worth a clean desk.

My THIS- Having an organized office. **My THAT-** organizing

That type of short check-in is not used by everyone but I have noticed that the people who take time to communicate and simply say this is where I am, this is where I am going and this is the help I might need, are the ones who most often achieve their goals.

Why? I believe that when you are accountable to someone you look up to it is much easier to pick up the pace and achieve your goal. An example is having a running partner -- it's hard to say, "not today" when they are ready for a run. You begin to realize that while you are responsible for your results someone is going to check on you if you are not having any.

A good leader or mentor is an excellent person to work with because you know they have your best interests at heart and are generally protecting you from any self-sabotage you might inflict. If you do not trust them to be selfless, if they are not willing to prod you along with grace and wit, you probably need someone else to help you.

This is too important of a role to give to someone who will not fill it with energy and compassion, so be choosey. It's okay. It's your goal and your excuse for success. They are along on the ride to support *you*.

As you have undoubtedly gathered by now I truly believe it is easier to achieve any goal when you know you have people in your corner. There is something else I believe makes achieving easier. Being in the corner for someone else.

In life you get what you give and if you give pure joy at the success of another person you are going to feel that pure joy yourself. Stop for a moment and list who you can help. Is it a new sales person, a student, someone struggling to get by? Who do you know that wants a goal you have achieved or is undertaking a new goal? I have a feeling they would be very grateful for a helping hand if it was offered to them. It does not take much time and it does not take perfection or supreme knowledge. All it takes is a willing spirit and the generosity to give them a boost when they need it.

I can help:

Because:

It is said that in teaching we do the best learning. We examine what we do or what we know and then explain it in the most generous and simplest terms to another. This act of giving knowledge makes the lesson stick with us.

I have always admired our Native American cultures. They wholeheartedly believe in passing down their knowledge in a "hands on," mentoring manner. It brings the generations closer and makes the teacher wiser and more able to help the next student. As you achieve success, pass it on. It's a gift to both you and the recipient.

Working toward your goal while accepting and offering help to others is what the theory of abundance is all about. It is living life by the golden rule and it is just the right thing to do. Sometimes though, life has unwelcomed twists. Let's discuss reality next.

What's Your Excuse?

Chapter 11

Reality

I almost hate to say it, but from time to time you are going to do every step, you are going to celebrate others, you are going to have the right goal and you are going to do the work you know needs done. You'll be rolling right along and life is going to step in and thumb its nose at your plan.

It's okay.

If it is grief, be in it. If it is illness, be ill. If it is joy, embrace it. We are given these times in our life so we can be alive. Fully experience them. In fully experiencing them you can still move forward in most cases. You have seen tremendous stories of people who conquer the insurmountable task while feeling life's pain. People find an inner strength when challenged and I think it is easiest to tap that strength if you have a solid plan.

One story I treasure is about a beautiful young woman, Nancy. Nancy was running a hundred-mile ultra-marathon through the dessert. Not yet half way through the race, at mile 47, she succumbed to dehydration and heat exhaustion, falling onto the gravel trail.

Nancy went to the medical tent for aid and soon heard Hans, a 65-year-old friend from Germany who was also running the race, as he bent by her side. Hans said, "Get up Nancy." Nancy laid there. Hans said "Nancy, get up." She could not.

"Nancy," he said in his thick, mature, German accent "in life there are good experiences and there are learning experiences. This is a learning experience, now get up Nancy."

Nancy finished the race.

From time to time everyone needs a coach, a friend, or a complete stranger to say, "Get up, Nancy." Or, someone to kindly say, "Your goal matters to me." I hope you will let Han's message ring in your ear. "There are good experiences and there are learning experiences." There will be times you will feel defeated like Nancy. It's okay, feel the pain. But get up and move forward.

If you just can't get up, when success is impossible and you miss the goal completely, publicly acknowledge you failed. Tell why you failed, don't give a lame excuse, and don't hide. It was a learning experience, it's okay. Tell the real reason you did not achieve the goal and smile because you tried.

I want you to know this: sometimes when you fail to meet a goal you have your best moments. One young man I know calls it failing happy. He says, "I might not make it to the top of the mountain, but I am going to sit in the middle of the mountain, enjoy the view and smile at my effort." It almost makes me want to go for a hike and fail happy, how about you?

So, if you fail, look the camera in the lens and say, "I didn't make it because..." and then take a breath. A hard breath, and say "but this is what I am doing about it," or "this is what I am doing next time." When you succeed or when you fail those around you learn from you. Be a role model no matter your results, people look up to you. Your brain looks up to you and it is your responsibility to be honest and show your fans and your brain how it's done.

You don't sit down and you don't wallow in failure. There is no time for that. You move forward, just move forward, your brain and your life will naturally follow. Set a goal, work for that goal, achieve it or don't. The cycle makes you a success because:

You do it again.

And you do it again.

And, suddenly you find you have an improved life. You are meeting goals and you are designing your life in your way. You become more you and you inspire someone else to become more them. Enjoy the feeling. Soak in the Jacuzzi when it is offered and be proud of the success you are achieving.

Sometimes it happens that when success rolls in someone else is jealous. Someone might stick a pin in your happy balloon or rain all over your parade. Unfortunately, it happens from time to time. What you do with their reaction is your choice. It can be your excuse for failure or your excuse for success.

What's Your Excuse?

I once coached with a sales person who lived in a very small town. Sue set goals and worked hard and achieved new levels of success. She bought a new car and went on trips she earned. She had a new hair style and she felt just amazing about who she was. Her faith had not changed. Her marriage was stronger, her kids had new clothes and her pride was visible.

Sadly, a friend who just loves to rain on parades spoke up. "Don't you think you're getting a little too big for your britches, Sue?" (Yes, she said that! Too big for your britches…. well, buy new britches is what I say! Live it up!) The friend then went on to say, "I mean with the car, the hair, all of the gallivanting about, who do you think you are?" Can't you just imagine her tone of voice and the way Sue must have felt when she heard that question? It must have been so deflating.

You see, success in their home town was to be achieved by men, not women. Success was to be good crops and kids that finished high school. Sure, you could win a ribbon for the best pie at the fair, but winning two years in a row was getting a bit uppity. Sue was breaking the norm and it was causing a bit of a stir, shall we say.

Sometimes, that is just the way it is. People are bitter and they are jealous and it is their thing, not yours. You can be a role model. You should be a role model. Invite them for a ride in your new car. You can even invite them to do what you are doing to earn this success. Hopefully they will join you; probably they won't.

Do it anyway, be a success, break the norm. Your kids are watching and so are theirs. There is someone who wants what you are achieving and they are learning to set goals and achieve those goals because that is what you, their role model does.

People who rain on happy parades are living their excuse. They are often unhappy with their lot in life or scared you might leave them. So, if someone says, "You are getting too big for your britches." Give them a big hug while saying "I know, it's crazy isn't it! I'd love to share my success with you because no matter what I achieve, you are always going to be in my life." That is usually what they are afraid of, that you and your success will leave them in the dust. And you won't.

Unless you should.

Part of the reason some people have had a hard time achieving goals is there, sadly, are people in their life who do not want them to achieve goals. Those people are happy with things just the way they are. Change is scary to them and the goal achiever is changing right before their eyes so they feel threatened. I've seen this happen with people who set a goal once and didn't make it. The failure reaffirmed in their minds what they already assumed to be true -- they were not a goal setter. Goal achieving was for other people. The result of that little experiment is they "settled" and part of what they settled for is to suck the ever-living life right out of others.

If you have someone who is trying to limit your growth leave them aside if you should, or care for them lovingly if you must. Just don't let them be your excuse for failure.

If you find that it is hard to work through situations like this on your own, get help. Enlist a therapist or a life coach. Talk to your pacing partner or work with a mentor. Make sure you have someone who has your back, especially if there is someone raining on your parade.

That is what a coach does. They ask questions and they care about your success. They let you solve your own problems and they encourage you to be more of yourself today than you were yesterday. A good coach does not let you wallow though. Sure, bad things happen, life stalls from time to time. A good coach acknowledges that fact and supports you as you move forward.

The cycle of doubt and success a goal achiever faces can be bigger than one person alone so don't do it alone. Ask someone to watch your back, to give you strength and assist in the heavy lifting of moving forward. It's not weakness; it's wisdom. Find a Hans to inspire you to brush off your fanny and keep running. As you gain experience and confidence you can pass it on to others. The theory of abundance sets in. You live your life as if to say, "I am having a good day and I want you to have a good day too." Let it flow.

That is what my small-town friend, Sue, did. She continued to run her business, she continued to see the world on trips she earned, she joyfully moved to a bigger city and she smiled a bigger smile. She met new people and her life continued to expand. All that happened for her because growth was her goal and her WHY was bigger than any negativity thrown her way.

I assure you, if you set the right goal, find the right excuse for success, then do the work, you will achieve your goals time and again. You will be an achiever because now you make a new kind of excuse. The right excuse and it is an excuse for success that is bigger than any trouble reality can throw at you.

As you have gone through this book you have had the opportunity to think about who you are, what you want to be, what holds you back and what can propel you forward. I have a feeling you have grown in the process and if not grown, at least have a new way of looking at your defining goals. I am not going to tell you *What's Your Excuse* and a new, thought filled style of goal setting will change your life completely. Generally, I don't think most people need their lives changed completely. I think they need their lives enhanced.

That is what we discuss in the final chapter, an idea for what you can do as a goal setter to enhance the life you are living now.

What's Your Excuse?

Chapter 12

Your DIDS list

As you probably know by now, I am a person who embraces a variety of experiences. I don't have a favorite team, a favorite wine, or an assigned chair at the dining room table. Why? Because I believe if you get too locked into one way of thinking, one way of doing, or one way of living you miss out on the best of life. Habits and tradition are wonderful but I balance them with challenge and the feeling of 'what's next' that keeps me feeling alive, growing, and invigorated.

I've owned several businesses, lived in several states, had lively conversations with an Astronaut, a Hacky-Sac World Champion and a cleaning woman who has happily cleaned the restrooms in one hotel... for 22 years. I've backpacked, stayed in 5 star hotels, and seen midnight Aurora Borealis while swimming in a river at 32 degrees below zero. It is a lifestyle that works for me, I am happy.

What I want you to think about now is what you really want. What makes *you* happy? Is your defining goal, as laid out in this book, to enhance your life or radically change it? Are you someone who wants to break their frozen hair while watching Aurora Borealis or do you want to work 8 to5 and live in the same house your whole life? Do you relish adventure or do you want to know exactly what each day will look like? Either plan is fine; I just want you to check in with your goal to assure it fits you, and who you want to be.

As I said at the close of the last chapter, I don't think most people need their life completely changed. If you live in fear or if you live a life that is not healthy, then you need a radical change, qualified assistance and this book is not the help you need; I wish you the best and pray for you.

If your goal is a big lifestyle change, a move to another country or exchanging one career for another, those are radical changes but your base experience is probably going to stay pretty much the same. You have relationships that work, bills that need paid and you probably know your favorite brand of catsup.

There is nothing wrong with comfort and if you have it, embrace it. Whether you are comfortable or not, enhancing your life would not be a bad thing, and achieving a defining goal will do just that- give life a bit of the zip or satisfaction you are seeking.

I know people who say they have big dreams, often they talk and talk; professing that someday they will build the house of their dreams or bike across the continent like Edvin and Emil. Some day they will hike the Grand Canyon, see the pyramids, *and* write an

Oscar winning screenplay. While absolutely achievable, these statements don't work as goals because the talkers aren't willing to do the first thing to achieve them, they are big dreams.

Big dreams are just fine, but imagine how wonderful life would be if you have met several defining goals and you possess a big list of DIDs.

What's a list of DIDs? Well, it is all the small things that make life interesting. DIDs are little challenges and little changes that keep you from being stuck in a rut. Your list of DIDs does not have to contain big things like swimming the English Chanel or circumnavigating the world alone, those are defining goals. Your DIDs should be things like baked a soufflé or walked every street in your neighborhood. Maybe you held a new-born for the first time, or tried painting with watercolors. My husband changed a tire at 20 degrees below zero and two months later he changed another tire at 113 degrees. Not fun DIDs to be sure but they are on his list because he said yes to two crazy road trips.

I believe your DIDs list is important to your growth and your happiness. It can challenge you, keep you fit, keep you interesting, and keep you thinking. People with big lists of DIDs never run out of things to talk about over the dinner table thus they avoid slowly becoming one of the silent couples you see in restaurants. Talking about the crazy sandwich you ate or the really strange art exhibit you took in at lunch is better than wondering if you have to discuss the same old argument one more time.

When was the last time you DID a road trip? What DID you do last night? What are you talking about with the people you love?

Many times, people limit the size of their experience or DIDs list because they watched TV, felt fat, or spent money foolishly. A DIDs list can also be limited by mindless pursuit of a singular goal. If you focus too long and too hard on just one thing you run the risk of being boring. You also run the risk of utter despair if you don't achieve that singular goal.

DIDs keep you interesting and they keep you learning, they may even make you brave.

I recently judged a speech contest for high school students. One young man, from a small Montana town, told us of a wonderful family tradition of eating at the same restaurant every Saturday night. They sit in the same booth, he eats the same meal each week and they talk about what is going on in their lives.

While the tradition is wonderful, giving these children a stable family experience, it is also limiting. He told us this story in an impromptu speech contest because he was scared and didn't know what else to talk about. He admitted it was his first time away from home and he felt completely lost, unable to concentrate without his customary meal on Saturday night.

I could not help but wonder what will happen when he goes to college or if he will even feel confident enough to leave home. I tried to engage him in conversation, but it was hard, he just wanted to be home.

When you have a big DIDs list, which this young man did not, you can talk about life; you can ask an acquaintance a question and have something to offer in return. You can stay in a hotel, read a map and you know that the best part of getting lost is the moment when you figure out where you are. DIDs make you stronger, braver, and more self-assured.

It's not hard to have a big DIDs list. Try watching a different sport this weekend. How about reading a different author tonight? Tomorrow, take a different route to work. This week, eat at a new restaurant. Your DIDs could be a bubble bath on Thursday or it might be taking your kids to a different city park each week this summer.

As you move through the day and the week DIDs become a bit of a challenge you can use for growth. Ask yourself 'do I want this to be on my DIDs list?' Sometimes simply having a list makes you talk to one more person, walk one more block, or stop and do the things that are on the HOW list of your defining goals.

In *What's Your Excuse,* we have focused on your defining goal. Achieving a goal large enough to need a WHY a HOW and a due date. Your DIDs can help you achieve your defining goal because the little DIDs help you move past your failure excuses.

By achieving and experiencing smaller, fulfilling events you become accustomed to success and achieving goals. Your defining goal looks that much easier when viewed through the eyes of someone who completes small goals or DIDs. Think of Edvin and Emil, exhausted, pedaling uphill, being passed by cars, trucks, and American RV's. When the downhill sign appeared in the distance they said, "Let's get to that sign and take a rest." Edvin hugged the goal, Emil snapped the picture and their DID helped them move one mountain closer to the west coast.

As you make your defining goal a priority simply choose a lot of little goals to go alongside your experience. You can do it. I challenge you to see how many things you can add to your DIDs list this week.

That is what the successful goal achiever does to maintain the ability to reach the next big goal, they choose a defining goal, then work towards it. Along the way they scoop up experiences and smaller accomplishments, DIDs, savoring those successes as they move onward.

Take a moment and reflect on the people you look up to. You may *personally know them, you may not, yet they justly deserve your* attention and admiration because of something they accomplished, a goal they set out to achieve.

They may be unsung heroes or they may be a name everyone knows, yet you find their story speaking to you. Do you want to be like them? Do you want to help them achieve their next goal, perhaps letting their defining goal in some way be your defining goal?

This often happens with big charitable drives and your goal is not negated because it piggybacks on someone else's. Do you recognize some of the smaller goals (DIDs) the people you admire achieved while working towards their defining goal?

Chances are you have more than one person to admire, and the things you admire about them are incredibly diverse. Undoubtedly their success has given you a vision for your success. Reflect on who they are and what their story means to you.

Who do you admire? How long have you admired them? What did they do to earn your admiration?

I admire_____, Because:

It's wonderful to have someone you admire, isn't it? I have an ever-growing list, and it includes obvious choices like people who overcome every roadblock that is against them to conquer the mountain, change society, or improve their own circumstances. I admire children who are too young to vote, yet who have enough wisdom and compassion to develop charities that help other people. I admire families who go through hardship and yet persevere to find a way to work and stay together.

My list also includes things that are less heralded, yet no less powerful such as women who nurture families while still making an impression on the world and men who bend down on one knee to teach a child how to accomplish a task.

I've found that when you look out at the world through eyes of expectation and happiness you see many amazing things, many amazing people, and many things you can choose to do. So many in fact it can be hard to settle in and say, "This is what I am doing, this is who I am." And yet, when you set out on the quest to achieve your defining goal that is what you want, to be able to say, "This is who I am."

My wish for you is accomplishment. I want you to be able to say "Hey! This is ME!" "I've accomplished my goal and I am happy!" I want you to be the person on someone else's list when they are asked who they admire. I want you to know completion, satisfaction, power, and pride.

Most importantly I want you to know that you are enough. Yes, just as you are right now is enough. Everything you possess is everything you need, you are who you are and you are becoming who you will be. You have set a goal that will define you, a goal that you want to achieve.

You have thought it through, declared it, mapped it out, and even chosen your excuse for success. Everything you truly need to accomplish that goal is in your head, in your heart and in your hands. You are exactly enough to achieve your goal.

Now all you must do is put one foot in front of the other and begin. There is more satisfaction in beginning, in trying, than in thinking about beginning, so take your first step right now. It's time. Begin.

Be aware as you begin, this is when excuses for failure can slip back in, the excuses that have kept you from achieving your goal in the past. You are not too old, too fat, too dumb, too broke, too tied down, too uncoordinated, or too busy to achieve your goal. Lay those doubts aside. You are enough.

If you are worried that any one of those or a myriad of other "too" excuses is going to slow you down talk with your support person. You could also watch an inspirational video, or read a story by someone with your same "too" fear who achieved their goal. If you are like me, after watching a few videos you will laugh at your excuse for failure and you will cry with joy as you watch other people achieving. It is beautiful.

Their story can be your story. All you must do is begin. Simply move towards your goal by accomplishing one DID today.

Your goal might not be to design a charity that changes the world; it might be to learn to dance. You may not aspire to be President of the United States; you may just want to learn to fly a plane. It is your goal, however, and it is your right -- no, it is your duty -- to protect it, nurture it and achieve it.

That is why you took time to choose your excuse for success, so you can achieve your defining goal. Achieving your goal is going to be wonderful. I know you can achieve it and so much more.

Simply:

- Declare a defining goal
- Know the WHYs, HOWs and due date of that goal
- Choose the right excuse; your excuse for success
- Enlist support while sharing your knowledge and gifts
- Be a goal achiever
- Cheer for yourself and others! Life is good when you do what you set out to do
- Shampoo, rinse, repeat

So, I ask you, what's your excuse?

What's Your Excuse?

Thank You

Thank you to Laura for editing, editing, editing, and praising. I could not have written this book without your loving support. Thank you to Rus who said "engaging" when he probably meant, you need to edit. Thank you to mom who edited- by hand! Thank you to Dawn who was the first one to really coach me into being an author. Thank you to Paul, Liz, Nick and Al who supported me through days, locked in a room, while I wrote and they ran our crazy wonderful life.

Thank you mostly to you, reader. Someone once posed the question- 'without someone to buy and read your book, are you really an author?' You helped me to lay that question to rest. I am an author and it feels crazy, wonderful, and scary and like I got over my own excuses.

Now, go live your defining goal. You can do it...and it will feel grand! ~Karen

What's Your Excuse?

Made in USA - Crawfordsville, IN
74245_9781521433546
03.22.2023 1814